# Table of Contents

I0436399

Dodo

Cape Verde Giant Skink

Deinosuchus

Tyrannosaurus Rex

Roque Chico De Salmor

Domed Rodrigues Giant Tortoise

Stellar Sea Cow

Plesiosaur

Asteroid

The International Union for the Conservation of Nature (IUCN)

Climate change

# EXTINCT

## Volume 1

## Seamus Shell

Digital Edition V1.0

seamus.shell@optusnet.com.au

# EXTINCT

## Volume 1

# Introduction

Creatures started to become **extinct** long ago, in the far distant past, going back to when the first dinosaurs made their appearance on the earth, some 230 million years ago in the Triassic Period; we can trace the evolution of these creatures from the fossil records which have been discovered in Argentina and Brazil.

The earliest known dinosaur was known as Eoraptor or "dawn hunter" which was 1 meter in length, and had the ability to be able to run very fast. From this beginning, dinosaurs evolved, becoming more adapted to their environment even during periods of climatic changes.

To-day over 700 species of dinosaurs have been named. Why the dinosaurs along with numerous other creatures on Land, Sea, and Air disappeared is an ongoing study for the scientists. Various theories, such as sudden climate change, volcanic eruptions, to a giant asteroid striking the earth are suggested for these creatures becoming extinct. Huge volcanic eruptions which unleased volcanic ash and poisonous gases into the atmosphere, blotting out the sunlight and effecting the process of photosynthesis, which plants require to grow, the food source of the herbivorous animals died out. The herbivorous dinosaurs had to eat 200 to 300 pounds of plant life every single day and when the climate changed this affected the smaller animals as well who got fitter and more agile in search of food.

The carnivorous animals such as Tyrannosaurus Rex or T-Rex also suffered because the smaller animals they used to hunt or scavenge for had become either very scarce or extinct and consequently their food supply dwindled.

Another popular theory among some scientists is that an asteroid such as the one that struck the Yucatan Peninsula in Mexico, causing an enormous crater about 180 kilometres or 111 miles wide, would have caused dust to blot out the sunlight like the volcanic eruptions did, and causing extremely cold weather for months or years. So whether it was climate change that made the climate drier and colder, volcanic ash or an asteroid blotting out the sun effecting the growth of plants, or a combination or all of them contributing to these creature becoming *extinct* is still open to debate.

One thing that is certain is that interference by humans upon creatures living before about 4 million years ago, either by hunting, or interfering with the habitat of these creatures did not occur, simply because humans did not exist before this time of 4 million years ago. The effect that man has had on the creatures that existed on earth since his appearance, is also outlined in this book **"EXTINCT"**

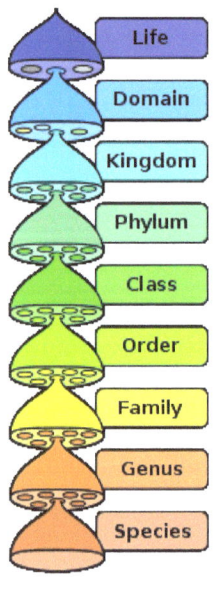

Biological classification's eight major taxonomic ranks, which is an example of definition by genus and differentia. A genus contains one or more species. Intermediate minor rankings are not shown.

# EXTINCT!

## Volume 1

## Seamus Shell

# Chapter 1

# EXTINCT

## Volume 1

# Animals

## Barbary Lion

Sultan the Barbary lion, at the New York Zoo. Photo courtesy Nelson Robinson 1897

The Barbary lion or Atlas lion became extinct in 1922 as the last known species was shot by hunters. Sultan the Barbary lion pictured above by Nelson Robinson in the New York Zoo in 1897 is regarded as the largest and the heaviest species among lions as males could weigh as much as190 to 230 kg or between 410 and 580 lbs. They generally hunted alone rather than in packs owing to the scarcity of food. They were extremely ferocious and had immense body strength. They were used in the Coliseum in Rome to amuse the crowd as they attacked the Gladiators. At the top of the food chain, this predator had no peers, and it's no wonder that the lion is known as the "King of the jungle".

Indiscriminate hunting with high powered rifles and a dwindling food supply led to the extinction of this magnificent animal. Although the Barbary lion is extinct in the wild, there are a few lions held in captivity which are descended from the original Barbary Lion. A selective breeding programme using DNA fingerprinting May 'breed back' this lion which if successful would see the lions released into the National Park in the Atlas Mountains of Morocco.

# Caspian Tiger

**Caspian Tiger** (*Panthera Tigris Virgata*), **Persian Tiger** (Berlin Zoo, 1899)

Distribution of Caspian Tiger

The Caspian tiger or Turan tiger was found in the region near the Caspian Sea. They were once among the biggest felids that ever existed. The image above is in the United States public domain because its copyright has expired by more than 70 years. The Caspian tiger was slightly smaller in size compared to Siberian tigers but were extremely powerful nevertheless. A male could weigh up to 235 kg or 518 lbs. inhabiting a wide area around the Caspian Sea, including Iran, Turkey, and Central Asia and extending into China. The main reasons for their extinction are destruction of habitat and indiscriminate poaching. The exact date of extinction is not known because some people believe it to be in the 1940s while others think it to be in the 1970s.

# Tasmanian tiger

http://cas.bellarmine.edu/tietjen/images/Tasmainian_wolf.jpg 1933

Thylacinus in Washington D.C National Zoo, 1906 Author E.J. Keller.

The Tasmanian wolf or Tasmanian tiger as this carnivore is most popularly known is a native animal of Australia, in particular Tasmania. It was one of the largest carnivorous marsupials in modern times. It has a close relative in the Tasmanian devil who is also threatened with extinction through a disease of the mouth. With the extinction of the Tasmanian tiger in 1936, the entire genus went into extinction. This thylacine was an apex predator as it had sharp predation skills relying mainly on sight and hearing. The distinctive black stripes are more prevalent at the back of the animal. The male thylacine had his genitals protected by a pouch from the thick undergrowth. From time to time there are supposed sightings of this Tasmanian tiger, but despite large rewards, no one has managed to capture or photograph one. One of the main causes of extinction of this species is believed to be the spreading of various diseases.

Between 1888 and 1909 the Tasmanian government paid 1 pound for each adult thylacine and ten shillings for thylacine pups. 2,184 bounties were claimed under this scheme. Hunting by wild dogs which were introduced by European settlers, the destruction of its habitat and distemper like disease all contributed to the extinction of the tiger. The Tasmanian government awarded official protection of the species on 10 July 1936, only 59 days before the last known specimen died in captivity. A case of too little, too late!

# Golden Toad

US fish &wildlife service, Bufo_periglenes1.jpg002.

The golden toad was endemic to the regions of Costa Rica especially the high tropical forest region above Monteverdi. This amphibian was one of the most beautiful toads with a golden orange colour. The females had red spots circled by yellow rings on a dark coloured body.

Not much is known about these beautiful creatures because they lived underground and only appeared around April each year as the wet season started. The males would wait for the females around puddles of water and after mating the females would lay over 200 eggs in these puddles. After a gestation period of about 8 weeks the eggs gave way to tadpoles.

They became extinct in the year 1989 and the main reason for their extinction was habitat loss and Chytrid fungus called chytridiomycosis. This fungus has a tendency to harden the skin of amphibians and therefore prevents respiration. In 2007 it was discovered that probiotic bacteria could prevent the disease chytridiomycosis from attacking amphibians. The Panama Amphibian Rescue and Conservation Project had been set up to rescue species in eastern Panama from this disease. Zoos and aquariums around the world named 2008 the year of the frog, to help draw attention to the plight of this amphibian.

One frog called Cochranella antisthenesi is endemic to Venezuela and is particularly sensitive to climate change. It inhabits the subtropical or tropical moist lowland forests and rivers and is also threatened with habitat loss. Climate change and the dry conditions which El Nino produced are the reasons that chytrid fungus thrived along with the lowering of the PH levels of the water are all reasons given for the recent extinction of the golden toad. Their golden colour fascinated everyone who saw them as this florescent amphibians skin glowed in the light.

# Western Black Rhinoceros

Photographed by Brocken Inaglory in: Ngorongoro Crater, Tanzania 28 October 2007

The western black rhino was a sub species of the Black rhino, and was declared extinct recently in 2011 by the International Union for the Conservation of Nature (IUCN). It was once found extensively in Africa; however indiscriminate poaching was the reason their population declined which ultimately led to extinction.

With the help of conservation measures, their population soared, but with the eventual decline in conservation efforts meant the hunters took undue advantage. While there were several hundred thousand rhinos living in Africa around 1900, however, this number had been reduced to 70,000 in the late 1960s to only 10,000 in 1981. By 2004 the number had declined to 2410, and by 2002 only 10 remained in Cameroon. Extinction was declared in 2011 by IUCN.

Black Rhinos were very aggressive and would even charge at tree trunks and termite mounds. 50% of males and 30% of females die from fighting. They can run at speeds up to 55 kilometres or 34 miles per hour. Being an herbivorous browser the black rhinoceros would eat leafy plants, thorny bushes and fruit. It can survive for 5 days without water. Both males and females urinated on bushes and around watering holes as a means to identify each other. This was to help compensate for their poor eyesight and maybe that is the reason they attack tree stumps. Breeding pairs can stay together for days or weeks and mate several times a day for a half hour each time. A single calf materialises after a gestation period of 15 to 16 months, and was the start of a 30 to 50 year (poacher free) life. A fully grown rhino had no predators, but the young could be taken by hyenas or lions.

Although it was bulky and extremely powerful the western black rhino was no match for the hunters with their powerful rifles and this proved too much for the species. A lax justice system which allowed illegal poachers to flourish led to the sad demise of this species!

Contributing to its extinction was Chinese demand for the horns which were composed of keratin. Superstitious beliefs that the horns when powdered and taken internally had an aphrodisiac effect on the consumer have been one of the main factors that have led to the demise of this magnificent creature. Desperate recent measures were taken to protect them from poachers, by cutting off their horns as a means to make them worthless. These extraordinary measures failed to save the western black rhino and it went the way of the Dodo, and was lost forever.

## Schomburgks Deer

Schomburgks deer was a native to Thailand, in particular near Bangkok; this species of deer resembles that of the Barasingha very closely. Herds consisting of one male, several females and their offspring, lived off shrubs and long grasses. Only the males had antlers, as only caribou and reindeer females have antlers. These antlers were used for fighting among the males, and for dominance and sexual displays.

The last species was killed in 1938. Their main reason of extinction is believed to be destruction of habitat as the open grasslands were converted into farms for raising crops such as rice. Not only this, but these animals were hunted extensively and were easy targets when clumped together on islands during the wet season. Both these reasons together cemented the rapid decline in population of this species leading to extinction.

# Caucasian wisent

An image of a killed Caucasian Bison from E. Demidoff's book 'Hunting Trips in the Caucasus'

Hybrid of *Bison bonasus bonasus* and *B. b. caucasicus* at the New Poznań Zoo, Poland. Author: Radomil_talk 3 May 2004.

Situated just north of the Russian resort of Sochi, the western Caucasus is unique in that it is the only large mountain area in Europe where human population has not encroached. A subspecies of the extremely powerful European bison, the Caucasian wisent became extinct due to the combined effect of inhumane hunting from poachers and from natural predators as well. Even the rapid loss of habitat contributed significantly to the problems of survival for this bison.

They were powerful enough to fight off small predators but their main danger was from animals like the Caspian tiger the Asiatic lion, as well as wolves and bears. It was poaching however that ultimately led to their downfall and even though there were approximately 2000 of them still remaining in the 1860's this number fell to only 50 by 1921. It was last seen in 1927 and is thus considered to be extinct.

# Quagga

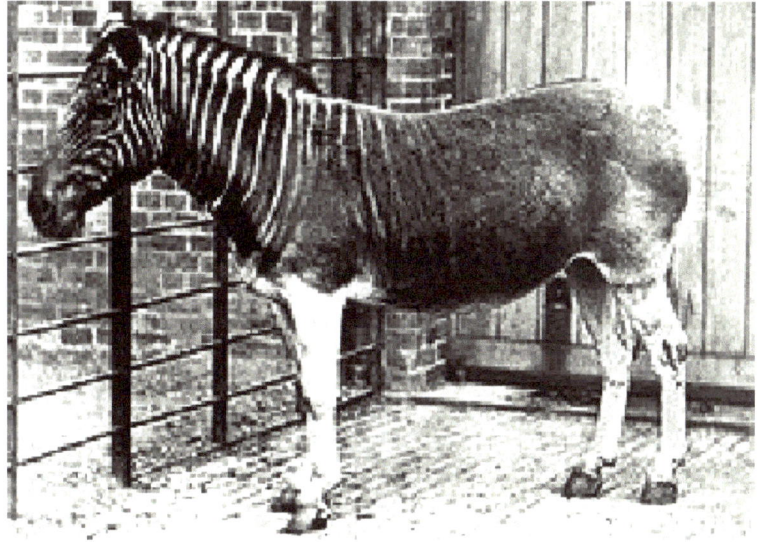

Quagga is an extinct sub-species of zebra. Mare, London, Regent's Park ZOO. F. York 1870. Once found abundantly in Africa, the Quagga is one of the most famous extinct species. It is a sub- species of the zebra. Having very distinct stripes on the front part of its body was what distinguished the Quagga from other Zebras.

The Quagga was widely hunted for its meat and its hide. It was last seen in 1883 and has been declared extinct ever since. They also resembled a horse. The photo above of a female quagga was the only photo ever taken of a live quagga at London's Zoo in Regents Park in 1870. It was the first extinct creature whose DNA was analysed and studied, and was categorized as a different species, however, before further research could be carried out, indiscriminate hunting of this animal led it to extinction.

# Mexican grizzly bear

Mexican Grizzlies (*Ursus arctos nelsoni*) at the Field Columbian Museum. 1919. Mills, Enos Abijah, 1870-1922. The Mexican grizzly bear was a species of brown bear, which has become extinct since 1964. These mammals were found in Mexico and were one of the largest and heaviest bears that were found there with some of the largest weighing over 325 kg or 715 lbs. Their fur had a silvery look and thus they were named the silver bear.

Its main diet consisted of plants, fruits and insects and sometimes it eat small mammals as well. This bear also fed on livestock from time to time and consequently were considered as pests by farmers. They were hunted, baited and shot without any regard for their preservation. Even after the species were declared endangered, the hunting continued and these bears inevitably went into extinction.

# Chapter 2

# BIRDS

## Black-faced Honeycreeper

Photos credit: Paul E. Baker/USFWS (U.S. Fish and Wildlife Service)

The Black faced honeycreeper or Po'uli as it is also known is a species of bird which was first listed as endangered but since no traces of the bird have been seen since 2002 it was declared to be extinct in 2004.

They were first discovered in 1973 and by the time they were found, their population had already dwindled to less than 200. They were an endemic species of Hawaii and inhabited the island of Maui. It fed on small insects and spiders.

Despite a massive effort by the State of Hawaii in establishing a 9,500 acre reserve connected to other protected areas, the Po'uli's numbers continued to decline until there were only 3 left by 1997. The main cause of their extinction apart from human interference has to be their low fertility rate.

# Elephant bird

Skeleton *Quaternary of Madagascar* by Monnier, 1913.

Aepyornis maximus. Author Acrocynus 4avril 2008

Elephant bird or Aepyornis maximus was found exclusively on the island of Madagascar. This bird is a species of flightless birds whose breast bones had no keel.

The famous explorer Marco Polo mentions very large birds during his explorations to the East in the 12$^{th}$ to 13$^{th}$ centuries, and it is believed that he was referring to the elephant bird. Aepyornis was the largest bird in the world, standing over 3 meters or 10 feet tall and weighing up to 400 kilograms or 880 pounds. However, owing to various hyper diseases from chickens these flightless birds were affected and suffered extinction.

Their eggs were extremely vulnerable as well, and eggshells were found in the charred remnants of human fires suggesting that humans made meals out of their eggs. These eggs were over a meter in circumference and had a length up to 34 centimetres or 13 inches. Compared to a chicken egg, you would be delighted to receive one for Easter, as it had a volume which was 160 times that of a normal chicken egg.

# Arabian Ostrich

Artist Syrischer Maler um 1335 The Yorck Project: *10.000 Meisterwerke der Malerei.* DVD-ROM, 2002. ISBN 3936122202. Distributed by DIRECTMEDIA Publishing GmbH.

The Arabian Ostrich lived near the Arabian Peninsula where it was once found extensively. However, later on with the onset of drought, these birds started withdrawing themselves from the Arabian Desert.

It is mentioned in ancient history especially Roman history where the ostrich featured in venatio or the hunt and this was a form of entertainment carried out in Roman amphitheatres. The great slaughter of wild animals such as Barbary lions as well as ostriches took place to entertain the masses at these venues.

The ostrich became a symbol of wealth for the rich. These birds suffered a lot after firearms were introduced as it made hunting them down extremely easy. By mid-20th century, this bird had nearly vanished as extreme hunting led to depletion of their count. The last ostrich was spotted in 1966 and it is declared extinct.

# Atitlan Grebe

Pied-billed Grebe (*Podilymbus podiceps*), Lake Patagonia (Arizona, USA), 2005; de: Bindentaucher. Author Mdf 2005. Photocopy of original. Made for G.R. Gray 1844.

The Atitlan Grebe (Podilymbus gigas) is a species of the grebe family of water birds and since it's extinction, the Pied-billed Grebe (Podilymbus podiceps) is the sole extant member of the genus Podilymbus. It was found locally in the Atitlan region in Guatemala.

Basically, it fed on small fish and crabs, however some other dominant species such as the largemouth bass which was an introduced species consumed these fish as well and thus the food source for this bird was further reduced. Dropping of the level of the lake and the removal of natural habitat by reed cutters may also have contributed to its demise. Although, care was taken to provide food to them, the earthquake that hit Guatemala in the 1970s further acted to hasten its extinction. Soon, their numbers kept dwindling until they became totally extinct.

# Passenger Pigeon

Photograph of a female Passenger Pigeon (*Ectopistes migratorius*) in captivity from the year 1898. J. G. Hubbard.

The Passenger Pigeon was a wild pigeon that existed freely in North America. It was once found in large numbers as estimated figures believe it to be in excess of 3.5 billion. However, excessive hunting and rapid destruction of habitat by conversion to farming, and deforestation finally reduced their numbers significantly and drove them to extinction.

They stayed together in flocks and such was the density of these migratory flocks that in 1866 one such flock was described as consisting of 3.5 billion birds that took 14 hours to pass overhead. Pigeon meat became popular as food for the slaves and the poor in the 19th century and this contributed greatly to their demise. However, despite being a strong social group, they became extinct in the 20th century. Martha was named as the last Passenger Pigeon who died in 1914 in the Cincinnati Zoo.

# Bush Wren

John Gerrard Keulemans (1842-1912): Photo (taken in 1911) of the South Island Bush Wren (Xenicus longipes longipes) Found in New Zealand, this bird was almost flightless. Blending into the natural bush habitat helped to camouflage the wren, however introduction of exotic species like rats, and mustelids wreaked havoc on the population of these birds. The bush wren had already started to disappear when they were last spotted in 1968. Their inability to fly made them even more vulnerable and extinction followed.

# Pink-Headed Duck

Distribution of records of Rhodonessa caryophyllacea, map generated using BirdSpot (birdspot.googlepages.com) using data from mainly BirdLife red data report records. The Pink-headed Duck (Rhodonessa caryophyllacea) was one of the most beautiful ducks that was found in the rivers of India, around Bangladesh, and the swamps of Myanmar. Measuring about 43 centimetres or 16.92 inches in length, the male had a pink bill, head and neck as opposed to the female which had a much paler pink around the head and neck and a darker bill. Their wings had a white leading edge to them. They had a two note call which sounds like 'wugh-ah'.

A peculiar thing about the pink-headed duck is that it laid spherical eggs not unlike the eggs of a tortoise. The last confirmed reports of seeing the birds were in 1935 and this led to it being categorized as extinct. Their pink coloured head made them stand out from other birds and they were sought after by hunters for ornaments because of their beautiful plumage. Although several reported sightings were made since it was declared extinct, they have not been substantiated. The reason for their extinction is believed to be loss of habitat, and hunting.

# New Zealand quail

New-Zealand Quail, (male and female)."Buller's "A History of the Birds of New Zealand, 2nd edition. Published 1888" Courtesy J.G.Keulemans

The New Zealand quail became extinct in 1875. It inhabited in various open lands and parks. It was once a common bird, however rapid destruction of habitat and natural predators together combined in making these birds extinct.

Although, they have striking resemblance to Australian quails, they are now considered to be a separate species after they were researched thoroughly. There were some problems with the phylogenetic classifications but with the studying of specimens, its closeness with other related species was monitored and it was categorized as a separate entity.

# Dodo

The dodo was a flightless bird which was endemic to the island of Mauritius. They became extinct by 1681 as most of them were killed by sailors and animals. People believed that this bird became flightless because it could easily get food on land and predators that could eat this bird were scarce at that time. Visiting humans brought animals such as rats, dogs and pigs with them to the island and it was these animals that reaped havoc on the nests of the dodo.

Deforestation by humans destroyed the habitat where the dodo lived. Flash floods were also thought to contribute to the demise of this bird.

Basically, most of the details about the dodo that we have are owed to paintings and written records from the previous era. Featured in Lewis Carroll's (Charles Lutwidge Dodgson) "Alice's Adventures in Wonderland" the dodo was immortalised as a caricature of Lewis

Carroll who because of a stutter would introduce himself as "Do-do-dodgson".

The dodo was thought to live on a diet of fruit, and it's only defence was its large beak which could inflict a nasty bite. They had no fear of humans and while they were not very palatable to eat this fearlessness and vulnerability contributed to their downfall as well. When someone wants to emphasise finality, or the fact that something is really dead, or extinct, no longer living, gone forever, they say "Dead as a dodo".

# Chapter 3

# REPTILES

## Cape Verde Giant Skink

The extinct Cape Verde Giant Skink (Chioninia coctei) Depiction from 'C. França: Le Professeur Barbosa du Bocage 1908.

The Cape Verde Giant Skink also known as macroscincus coctei inhabited the Cape Verde islands of the Atlantic Ocean. Owing to human destruction, these islands have now become deserts and are considered to be one of the prime causes of extinction. Although, this reptile was an herbivore, the lack of food source finally made it carnivorous as it would eat the young birds and eggs from the nests of birds.

It is believed that convicts were shipped to these islands and they used to consume these reptiles. An interesting fact about the giant skink is that they had a transparent lower eyelid presumably to see to see food from below. They were also hunted for their skink oil. After their dwindling numbers and then total decline, they were declared extinct in 1914.

# Deinosuchus

Photograph of
"*Phobosuchus riograndensis*" (*Deinosuchus rugosus*) skull reconstruction: the actual fossils are of a darker shade, while the majority of the skull is light-shaded plaster. Fossil discovered by Barnum Brown, restored by Roland T. Bird. 1954k

Salt Water Crocodile - the largest crocodile in the world. Image credit: Molly Ebersold, Wikimedia Commons, GNU Free License

Source: http://en.wikipedia.org/wiki/File:SaltwaterCrocodi...

Deinosuchus or terrible crocodile as it was known was the largest crocodile that ever lived. It measured up to 12metres or 39 feet in length and an adult crocodile could weigh between 8 and 9 tons. They became extinct about 75 to 80 million years ago and remained unknown until 1858 when their remains were first discovered. It lived in North America and is believed to be a great ambush predator. Its power was such that it could kill even massive animals with ease. It could lurk in water and stay hidden until its prey arrived to drink and then pounce upon it and consume it. Sea turtles, fish and even dinosaurs were all in the range of food sources for this terrible crocodile.

Compared to modern day crocodiles who have the a biting strength of 9,450 newtons which is the strongest bite of any living animal, the Deinosuchus had an awesome bite of 18,000 newtons lending weight to the suggestion that it also could possibly have included Tyrannosaurus Rex in its menu.

Crocodiles have a cerebral cortex and a four chambered heart. They have webbed feet which aid them in swimming and walking. The scales of a crocodile have sensory pores that secrete an oily substance that aids them to flush off mud. They don't have sweat glands so they like to rest with their mouths wide open to release heat, something like the way a dog releases heat by panting.

An interesting thing about crocodiles in general is that they can stay underwater for two hours at a time. It accomplishes this feat even though it does not have gills like a fish, by loading carbon dioxide in its bloodstream. When it flushes the carbon dioxide into its stomach, the digestive juices become very acidic, enabling the crocodile to digest the flesh and bones of its captured prey.

Crocodiles have long, narrow, V-shaped snouts, for capturing fish and small mammals, while alligators have wider U-shaped snouts, giving it more crushing power to capture turtles and larger animals that come to drink at the water's edge. The alligator has a wider upper jaw allowing the lower teeth to fit snugly into it, while the crocodile's jaws are the same width which allows the teeth to interlock.

Originally classified in the Crocodylidae family by Colbert and Bird based on dental features, a re-evaluation in 1999 by Brochu determined that Deinosuchus was a primitive member of the Alligatoroidea family and had features like those of the modern American alligator. Therefore, Deinosuchus was one of the largest Alligators that ever lived.

# Tyrannosaurus Rex

First restoration of a Tyrannosaurus (holotype CM 9380) skeleton ever published 1905 William D. Matthew

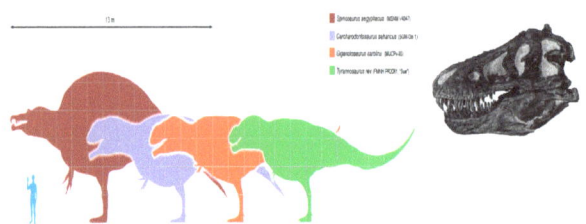

Complete Tyrannosaurus Rex skull, AMNH. A.E. Anderson                                      1912
http://digitallibrary.amnh.org/dspace/handle/2246/49

## Tyrannosaurus Rex,

Pencil drawing Nobu Tamura 26 Feb 2007

T-Rex is one of the largest known carnivores with a massive body size. They had amazing power and the very sight of one caused panic to lessor animals. The fossil records that were found for this species in North America confirm their existence 60 to 65 million years ago. They had a huge head and an amazingly long tail for balancing their movement. They roamed about freely in the regions of North America as they were at the top of the food chain with no threats, with the exception of the Deinosuchus or terrible crocodile that was the only creature capable of drowning this king tyrant lizard when it came to the river or water hole to drink.

T. Rex as it is sometimes called for short was a bipedal carnivore who tipped the scales at around 8 tons. Measuring up to 12.6 metres or 41.34 feet in length and 4 metres or 13 foot tall at the hips, it had a highly developed sense of smell that could sniff out dead carcasses miles away.

In 2012 scientific analysis using the latest laser beam technology on the fossil remains of these creatures concluded that these dinosaurs hunted in deadly blood-thirsty packs, and nothing that stood in their way stood any chance of survival.

It is not known for sure what the exact cause of extinction was with T. Rex and various theories put forth include climate change due to an asteroid hitting the earth, to shifting of the earth's crust with the resulting devastation to the plant life from tsunamis and volcanic eruptions creating dust clouds that blotted out the sun for months and consequently destroyed the food source that the dinosaurs relied upon.

The dinosaurs could have gone extinct simply because they grew too big. The herbivorous dinosaurs had to eat 200 to 300 pounds of plant life every single day and when the climate changed this affected the smaller animals as well who got fitter and more agile in search of food. The carnivorous dinosaur's food source declined and these almost mythical creatures became extinct.

# Roque chico de Salmor

Author J.Smit 1891

Roque chico de Salmor or giant lizard was present near El Heirro region in the Canary Islands. They resided in a small region and thus had a narrow habitat. However, indiscriminate hunting and collecting of these lizards as specimens for research work led to a sharp reduction in their number. They were even predated upon by gulls and feral cats

They totally disappeared in the 1930s which led to them being termed as extinct.

# Domed Rodrigues Giant Tortoise

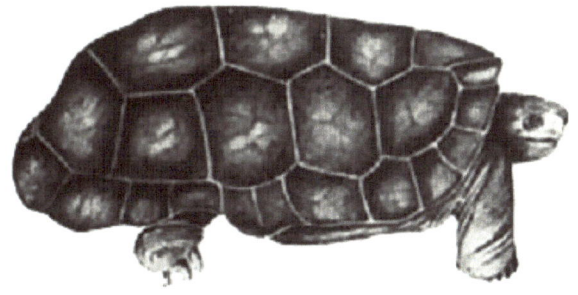

A

living Domed Rodrigues Giant Tortoise

(Cylindraspis peltastes) circa 1770 Jossigny.

These tortoises were extremely large and they belonged to the Testudinidae family of giant tortoise. It gets its name from its place of origin namely: Rodrigues, in the Republic of Mauritius. The last one was seen around 1800. Not much minute detail could be obtained for this specific tortoise owing to lack of proper specimens.

Sailing ships would pick them off the island and keep them as an additional food source during their voyages. The tortoise could survive for up to 14 weeks without eating or drinking. Up until the early 17th century only pirates exploited them until a journal of a Huguenot castaway drew attention to them. In this journal Francois Leguat wrote in 1691 that one turtle weighted a 100 pounds. Sailors said the meat of the turtle was sweeter than chicken and the word got around until its extinction in 1800.

# Chapter 4

# SEA CREATURES

## Stellar Sea Cow

Drawing of Steller's Sea Cow. Author: Georg Steller, date 1700s

The steller sea cow was the largest member of the sirenia order. It was initially found abundantly near the north pacific region surrounding the Commander Islands. Georg Wilhelm Steller first described it in 1741. Always living in the water, the steller sea cow fed mainly on a variety of kelp.

They were hunted down ruthlessly and it was the indiscriminate hunting of this species for food and for its skin which was used to make boats that led to its extinction. They could grow to as long as 8 meters and estimates that it could have weigh up to about 5000 Kilograms or 11,023 pounds. It was due to their bulky weight that they moved so slowly and were easy to capture. It was related to the present day dugong and manatees although it was much larger.

# Plesiosaur...

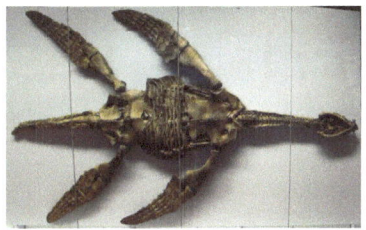

Museum Löwentor, Stuttgart, Germany.Author: Ra'ike 29 July 2008 Specimen # SMNS 12478

*Kronosaurus* hunting on the **plesiosaur** *Woolungasaurus. Dmitry Bogdanov 2000-2008*

The Plesiosaur named from the Greek: plesios meaning 'near to' and sauros meaning 'lizard' had a long neck, a short tail, and a body like a tortoise, and four fins. The plesiosaur can be described as a snake threaded through a tortoise. A lot of fossils have been discovered of this species. They were marine animals and could measure 20 meters or 65.6 feet in length. Only the sperm and blue whale grew larger than the plesiosaurs. A peculiar feature of the plesiosaur is that it had four-flippers, which is not seen in any modern animals.

There is speculation that the 'Lock Ness Monster' in Scotland could be a Plesiosaur. In 2004, an intact juvenile plesiosaur was discovered by a fisherman in Somerset, in the UK. Plesiosaurs had powerful jaws, with which to bite through hard shells such as molluscs. They could have eaten squid-like creatures as well. It is now known that they gave birth to live young since the discovery of a pregnant plesiosaur fossil. Gizzard stones or small rocks held in the gastrointestinal tract were used to help with digestion.

Plesiosaurs were common during the Jurassic period from 200 million years ago to the K-T extinction event about 65.5 million years ago, when dinosaurs, Mosasaurs, pterosaurs, and plesiosaurs, became extinct. It is thought by some scientists that an asteroid or a collection of asteroids crashed through the earth's atmosphere, and smashed into the earth leaving huge impact craters. Coupled with volcanic activity, the amount of dust and ash that was released into the atmosphere, would have blotted out the sun, and consequently prevented photosynthesis for the plants to grow. No food source for the smaller animals and fish meant no food for the dinosaurs and plesiosaurs which meant that they became extinct.

# Asteroid

Asteroid crashing into the sea. Created by NASA. Original up loader was Fredrik at en.wikipedia 18-05-2004.

About 65 million years ago during the Cretaceous-Palaeogene or the Cretaceous Tertiary period a mass extinction of plants, and animals occurred. The K-Pg or the K-T extinction derives its name from the fact that K stands for the Cretaceous and Pg for the Palaeogene period. During the K-Pg event dinosaurs, plesiosaurs, invertebrates of all kinds, as well as plants were suddenly wiped off a large portion of the earth.

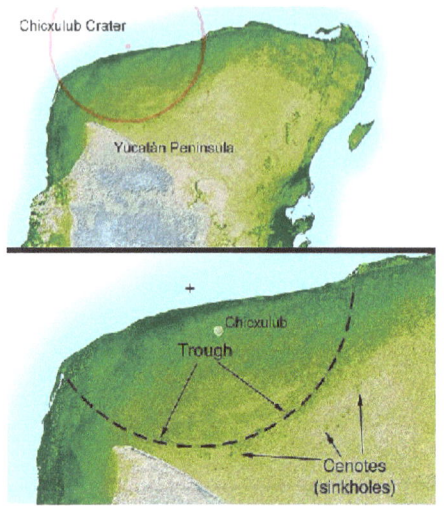

## Chicxulub Crater.

The Asteroid that struck the Yukatan Peninsula in Mexico formed a gigantic crater over 180 kilometres or 111.846 miles in diameter. The effect of an Asteroid plunging into the sea would create a monstrous tidal wave or tsunami which would have devastated life for hundreds of miles inland. Many scientists believe that several Asteroids crashed into the earth during this extinction period which resulted in many animals and sea creatures becoming extinct.

# The International Union for the

# Conservation of Nature IUCN

The International Union for the Conservation of Nature IUCN is providing the world with scientific information on the threatened state of biodiversity around the earth.

IUCN has a Red List which catalogues and highlights plants and animals that are under the threat of extinction. Species that are not included on the Red List are those that went extinct before 1500 AD. The aim of the Red List seeks to convey to the public and policy makers the urgent need of becoming aware of conservation problems and the importance of coming together as a global community to reduce <u>the extinction of creatures</u>.

The Species Survival Commission (SSC) has been working in conjunction with IUCN since 1963 in evaluating the conservation status of species, and in so doing bringing attention to those species and subspecies that are on the verge of extinction and also promoting their conservation.

In consultation and testing with more than 800 SSC members and other scientific bodies the Red List Categories and Criteria were adopted by IUCN in 1994. All bird species were evaluated in 1998 and in 1996 IUCN Red List documented the conservation status of every mammal species in the world. 5,205 species were evaluated in the 1996 list. By 2011 over 61,000 species on the Red List and all mammals, birds, amphibians, sharks, conifers and reef building corals had been assessed.

The vast variety of species which exist today took some 3.5 billion years of evolution. Of the estimated 14 million species in existence only about 1.8 million have been described. An amazing fact is that 25% of all the described vertebrates have their home in freshwater habitats which only cover 1% of the world's surface.

**Areas have been categorized:**

1a - strict nature reserve

1b - wilderness area

11 - National park

111 - Natural monument or feature

1V - Habitat or species management area

V - Protected landscape/seascape

V1 Protected area with sustainable use of natural resources

## Category 1a – Strict Nature Reserve

Strict nature reserves are designated to protect the geological and geomorphological features of the region and prohibit all but scientific study, environmental monitoring and education. Areas that have a special spiritual significance are also protected.

## Category 1b – Wilderness Area

**Wilderness areas** are large compared to other categories (except national parks which are of a similar size) and are devoid of human infrastructure. Visits by humans are allowed if they travel on foot or by boat. The only exception to this rule is that indigenous groups and their cultural and spiritual values are allowed.

## Category 11 – National Parks

National parks are similar in size to wilderness areas and are more liberal in so far as they allow human visitation and supporting infrastructure. Managed tourism is allowed so as not to reduce the effectiveness of conservation efforts. Vast areas of national park such as the **Serengeti** in Tanzania in Africa are a prime example of a national park. **Serengeti National Park,** in Tanzania is a designated Wilderness Area

Serengeti National Park in Tanzania

## Category 111 – Natural monuments

**Natural monuments** which have historical significance can be either of a natural nature or be introduced by humans including a site of a spiritual nature and its surrounding habitats. Examples of such natural monuments which include human introduction incorporating astronomy, and which also have a spiritual significance are the Pyramids of Egypt, Manchu Picchu in Peru, Stonehenge in England, and Newgrange in Ireland.

Newgrange is older than Stonehenge and older than the great pyramids of Giza having been constructed around 3200 BC during the Neolithic period. It had religious significance because it is aligned with the rising sun, which floods the inner chamber on the winter solstice.

According to the archaeologist Colin Renfrew, Newgrange is "unhesitatingly regarded by the pre-historian as the great national monument of Ireland" and it is also widely recognised as one of the most important megalithic structures in Europe.

# Newgrange in County Meath Ireland

Author of Newgrange mound above: Shira 18 March 2008

The mound is 76 metres or 250 feet across and 12 meters or 40 foot high, covering 0.4 hectares or 1 acre of ground.

Source own photo. Modifications by Locutus Borg.

Entrance at Newgrange with stone showing megalithic art.

The Neolithic people were agriculturalists and as they had not yet developed metal, so all their tools were made out of either, stone, antler, wood or bone.

Built between 3100 and 2900 BC, Newgrange is approximately 5000 years old. It is 500 years older than the Great Pyramid of Giza in Egypt, and is 1000 years older than Stonehenge in England.

# Category 1V - habitat or species management area

## The Galapagos, Ecuador

Author of the above photo: Datune at en.wikipedia 21 December 2007

The Galapagos islands situated off the west coast of Ecuador, come under a perpetual management area classification under which the prevention of poaching, creation of artificial habitats, halting natural succession and supplementary feeding practices may be implemented.

## Category V- protected landscape/seascape

Protected landscapes and seascapes is the most flexible of all the categories, and are able to accommodate ecotourism while maintaining historical management practices.

## Category V1 – protected area with sustainable use of natural resources.

**ICUN Category V1** focuses on developing a balance between nature conservation and sustainable development in conjunction with the livelihoods of those who are dependent on both.

### The Great Barrier Reef

Author: NASA Goddard Space Flight Centre's, NASA Visible Earth: Great Barrier Reef

# Climate change

Climate change is now talked about all around the world with governments of countries imposing a carbon tax on the Companies most responsible for polluting the atmosphere. Spewing pollutants out of their tall chimneys and the deforestation of forests are reasons for imposing a carbon tax on offending Companies.

Scientists are increasingly concerned that the climate is warming up with the consequent rise in sea levels. Already islands are being submerged by the rising levels of the sea. Low lying areas and land that is below sea level are in danger of being lost. Coastal areas all around the globe are seeing sea levels rise every year due to the melting of the ice-bergs.

Animals such as the polar bear have to swim longer and longer distances in the icy water to get from one ice sheet to the next in search of food. Specialized habitat and narrow environmental tolerances effect many creatures and climatic changes exposes their environment to sharp disturbances such as the melting of the ice or the destruction of the habitat in the case of water evaporation and the drying up of marches mangroves and lakes which were home to numerous species of birds and fish and frogs.

These changes can happen so quickly that the species that relied on the specialized habitat have not the ability to move to other areas or to colonize a new or more suitable area.

The logging and burning of the lungs of the earth; the tropical forests of the evergreen grasslands of the amazon are one of mankind's most stupid of errors. Not only is the natural habitat of numerous species being destroyed leading to the extinction of countless creatures, but the scientific analysis of all these creatures is put in jeopardy.

Moreover, the medicinal cures that the amazon forests hold are lost forever with the unrelenting logging of the trees. The slash and burn techniques are used to clear the forest for farming and to supply the fast food outlets, with beef. Cutting down a pristine forest which is home to thousands of creatures to allow cattle to be bred for the fast food outlets is a crime that we will all have to pay for.

When it is considered that around 40% of the oxygen in the earth's atmosphere comes from the forests of the Amazon River in South America, it could be concluded that mankind is on the path to self-extinction not to talk about the animals, birds, insects, and sea creatures becoming extinct.

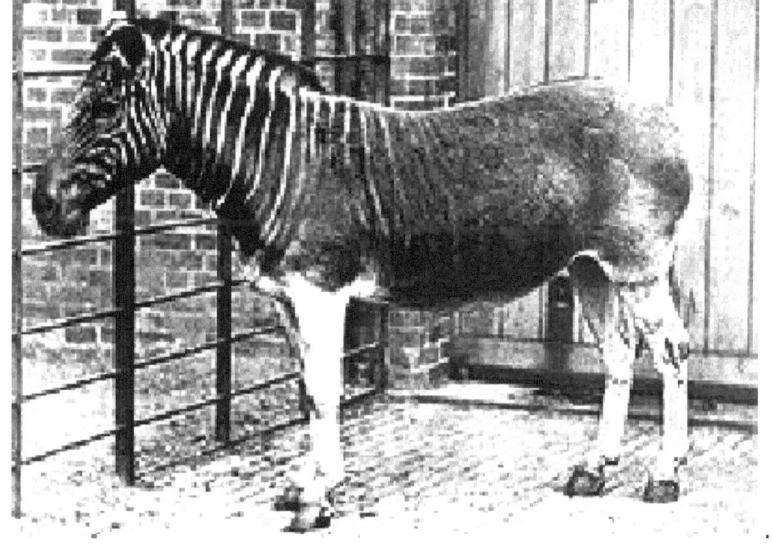

If you liked, "EXTINCT" volume 1

You'll love, "EXTINCT" volume 2
http://www.amazon.com/EXTINCT-ebook/dp/B0080K8G9E/ref=sr_1_cc_1?s=aps&ie=UTF8&qid=1336626842&sr=1-1-catcorr

Other books by Seamus Shell: "ZOO" for 5 to 10 year olds.

http://www.amazon.com/ZOO-ebook/dp/B007ZXQDV0/ref=sr_1_8?s=digital-text&ie=UTF8&qid=1336154156&sr=1-8